Hope lives
when people remember.

—*Simon Wiesenthal*

SIMON WIESENTHAL CENTER

BEIT HASHOAH

MUSEUM OF TOLERANCE

ABOVE: *The museum, from Memorial Plaza.*

FRONT COVER: *The innocence, hope, and flourishing culture of European Jews were destroyed in the Nazi death camps.*

INSIDE FRONT COVER–PAGE 1: *The museum's archives include many artifacts found at concentration camps.*

PAGES 2–3: *Memorial Plaza. A distinctive wall, engraved with names of Nazi death camps, ghettos, cities, and concentration camps, surrounds the plaza. The 18-foot menorah pays tribute to the rebirth of Jewish civilization after the Holocaust.*

BEIT HASHOAH ■ MUSEUM OF TOLERANCE
9786 West Pico Blvd., Los Angeles, CA 90035–4792 • (310) 553-8403

Albion Publishing Group
Lorie Bacon, Publisher
Santa Barbara, CA • (805) 963-6004

Project Editor: Anne Du Bois
Art Director: Joanne Station
Writer: Cheryl Crabtree
Copy Editor: Ann Merlin
Editorial Assistant: Suzanne Rode

ILLUSTRATION CREDITS

Adolf Hitler (Hamburg, 1936): 33 top. Leon Alligood/*Nashville Banner:* 11 left. AP/Wide World Photos: 22 bottom, 23, 43 top. Archives of the State Museum in Oswiecim: 26–27, 37 top. *Ein Bilderbuch für Gross und Klein* (Nuremberg, 1936): 30 bottom. Henry Block Collection/SWC Archives: Front cover. Bundesarchiv, Koblenz: 34, 35 top left & right. Dokumentationsarchiv des Österreichischen Widerstandes, Vienna: 33 bottom. David Hawk: 25. Kim Kulish/*Los Angeles Daily News:* 17. ME Design: Inside front cover–1. Jim Mendenhall: 2–3, 4, 12–13, 15, 16 bottom, 18, 19, 22 top (Courtesy Library of Congress), 24, 28, 29 bottom, 36, 38 top, 40–41, 43 bottom, 44-45, 47, 48, 49, back cover. Artwork by Arnold Schwartzman/SWC Archives: 6–7. Art Waldinger: 8, 9. SWC Archives: 11 right, 38 bottom left & right, 39, 42. Yad Vashem: 30 top left & right, 32, 35 bottom.

CONTENTS

INTRODUCTION
TOLERANCE THROUGH EDUCATION
7

THE TOLERANCENTER
A WORKSHOP OF HUMAN BEHAVIOR
13

BEIT HASHOAH
THE COURAGE TO REMEMBER
27

ACCESS TO HISTORY
45

INTRODUCTION

TOLERANCE THROUGH EDUCATION

■

The Simon Wiesenthal Center is a leading international Jewish human rights agency. Since 1977 it has fought against racism, bigotry, and intolerance around the world through education and social action. Named in honor of renowned Holocaust survivor and humanitarian Simon Wiesenthal, the Center has more than 380,000 member families and offices throughout the United States and in Canada, France, and Israel.

PAGES 6–7: *Detail of the poster for the Simon Wiesenthal Center's feature-length documentary,* Genocide, *produced by Arnold Schwartzman and Rabbi Marvin Hier. The film, which won an Academy Award in 1982, tells the story of the Nazi Holocaust through historical film clips and personal accounts of witnesses and victims. Video copies of this and other Simon Wiesenthal Center productions are available for purchase at the museum.*

The Simon Wiesenthal Center's myriad outreach programs and media projects focus on prejudice, antisemitism, and other human rights issues. The BEIT HASHOAH ▪ MUSEUM OF TOLERANCE is a natural outgrowth of the Center's commitment to education as a means of achieving its goals.

Rabbi Marvin Hier, founder and dean of the Center, determined two main purposes for the museum, as reflected in the dual nature of the major exhibit area.

Foremost is the urgent need to combat widespread intolerance and hatred to ensure a harmonious world for future generations. The **Tolerancenter** focuses on human behavior as it relates to the American experience. Multimedia exhibits help visitors learn how to recognize intolerance and how to stand up against it.

Beit Hashoah, or "House of the Holocaust," reminds future generations of the disastrous consequences of intolerance run amok, using the Nazi Holocaust as the ultimate example of man's inhumanity to man. It

LEFT: *The museum's ground-breaking ceremonies took place December 7, 1986. Holocaust survivors placed soil from Nazi death camps into the foundation, expressing hope in the museum's plan to educate people of all ages in the ways of tolerance. The museum officially opened February 8, 1993.*

serves as a vivid warning that intolerance, when given full reign, can lead to mass murder in the worst degree. The museum also honors Holocaust victims, righteous gentiles, and resistance fighters, and it preserves the memories of Jewish culture before World War II.

BELOW: *Holocaust survivor Robert Clary, speaking to a group of students as part of the Simon Wiesenthal Center's educational programs, shows the identification number tattooed on his arm by the Nazis.*

SOWING THE SEEDS OF HOPE

In December 1986 thousands of people participated in the museum's official ground breaking. Soil from World War II death camps was shipped to Los Angeles for the ceremonies. Hundreds of Holocaust survivors took handfuls of the soil and placed them carefully into the ground, sowing "seeds of hope" for a better world.

From these seeds has emerged the Simon Wiesenthal Center's BEIT HASHOAH ■ MUSEUM OF TOLERANCE. The eight-level, 165,000-square-foot complex opened its doors to the public in February 1993. Thousands of individual and corporate donations, as well as a grant from the state of California, contributed to its construction. With every visitor's journey through the museum, the seeds of hope take stronger root, and the possibility of a world without hate becomes more of a reality.

A Museum for a New Era

ABOVE: *Dr. Gerald Margolis is the director of the Simon Wiesenthal Center and of the* Beit Hashoah ▪ Museum of Tolerance.

OPPOSITE: *Prejudice and racial hatred appear in many guises, as illustrated by the angry faces of the Ku Klux Klan members in 1991, left, and the joyfulness of participants at a late-1930s Nazi rally, right.*

Tribalism. Ethnic strife. Racial hatred. Antisemitism. Unbridled prejudice. Violence. Genocide. These words haunt the course of human affairs of the past century. The prospect of a new century, however, offers us the opportunity to reassess our social environment and to establish an alternative dialogue of humane concern for others and a respect for human dignity. This is the mission of the museum in a new era—to explore alternative visions, to challenge set ideas and, ultimately, to question. The hallmark of this new dialogue might not necessarily be found in the answers we discover, but in the questions we are prepared to ask.

Primarily, these are questions of responsible citizenship in a local community, a national forum, or the world community. The same questions that can be asked of individuals can be asked of nations. What must be discovered for a new era is true moral purpose and commitment. What is a just and tolerant society? What allows for the fostering of human dignity? How do we guarantee the rights of the individual and the group within the context of the needs of the many? How do we avoid what is harmful? In short, we must be prepared to question ourselves in order to redefine ourselves and our world.

The Beit Hashoah ▪ Museum of Tolerance cannot claim that it will cure the world of prejudice and ethnic and racial hatred. The significance of the museum, however, is its direct and immediate confrontation with issues of human dignity and our relationship to others. The challenge of the museum is how it affects the minds and hearts of individuals and influences them toward positive change. It is an environment where the social dynamic of ethnic relations is explored and where our private perceptions of other people are provoked and questioned.

In every respect there has never been a more timely or urgent need for the Beit Hashoah ▪ Museum of Tolerance. A museum dedicated to preserving the memory of the Holocaust and teaching the lessons of this horrific event. A museum predicated upon understanding the remarkable multiethnic strands in America's social landscape. A museum of participation, contemplation, and dialogue. A museum of enduring value.

Gerald Margolis, Ph.D.
Director

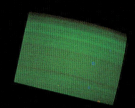

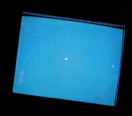

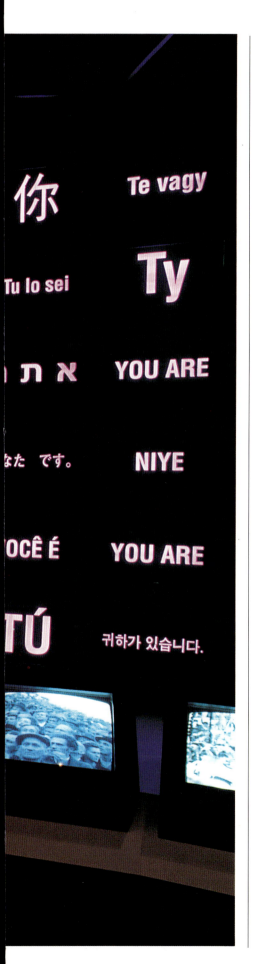

THE
TOLERANCENTER

A WORKSHOP
OF HUMAN BEHAVIOR

■

Throughout our lives we are bombarded with messages that reinforce negative attitudes toward certain people. These messages are the building blocks of hatred. When individuals with similar feelings band together, this hatred forms the basis of mass assaults and murders.

In the **Tolerancenter** you explore these messages as they relate to the American experience. This is not a place for observation at a distance. The exhibits emphasize active participation, which begins as you take your first steps toward the entrance.

PREJUDICED

UNPREJUDICED

PAGES 12–13: *A main Tolerancenter theme is individual choice versus the power of the media and persuasive people, such as demagogues. This theme is impressed upon you in the final multi-screen exhibit, the Persuaders, which features images of influential people and your friendly, but abrasive, Tolerancenter video host, the Manipulator.*

WATCH YOUR MOUTH

In the **We the People** corridor life-size images of Americans mingle with sounds of cheering, marching bands, children playing. You soon realize that the moving shadow on a football field or the silhouette behind a group of children is yours, underscoring your participatory role in American culture. This theme pervades the entire museum: that we, as individuals in a democratic society, are *each* responsible for its course through history.

WHO CONTROLS OUR THOUGHTS?

The **Tolerancenter** raises an important issue: the power of persuasive people and media images to influence our attitudes.

Your multiscreen video host, the **Manipulator,** is an ongoing reminder of this issue. In the entry hall he peppers you with compliments: "You're my kind of people—bright, sensitive. Remember, I like you!" His smooth voice and sugary smile offer a false sense of security, enticing you into a state where he can easily direct and control you. On some screens the **Manipulator**'s voice and face correspond to his subtle justifications of racism and bigotry. On others he scowls or contorts his expression to match underlying negative thoughts.

The **Manipulator** assumes he has caught you in his web of words and that you are now in his power. After shooing you through the entry doors, his voice echoes periodically in the exhibit area, constantly challenging and provoking your thoughts.

CHOICES AND CONSEQUENCES

At the **Tolerancenter**'s two entry doors, labeled **Prejudiced** and **Un-prejudiced,** you make the first in a series of choices. Do you really think you are completely without prejudice? If so, a surprise awaits you.

LEFT: *The Manipulator, your "charming" video host during your Tolerancenter tour, welcomes you. What is he* really *saying? Watch and listen . . . carefully.*

BELOW: *The Other America, a large map of the United States, shows that hundreds of hate groups exist throughout the nation. You learn the nature of particular groups and their current activities using a computerized touch-screen menu.*

ABOVE: *It's easy to make false assumptions based on stereotypes. A physically impaired man enters a social services building—to apply for aid, of course. But in this exhibit you discover that he's actually in charge of the office.*

BELOW: *Do we use stereotypes to categorize people? They can prevent us from seeing others as unique individuals.*

Next, a series of displays engages you in personal encounters with stereotyping, prejudice, and intolerance. The nature of prejudice and the connection between prejudiced thoughts and violent acts grow clearer.

Several exhibits explore the way we use superficial qualities to judge people. **Matching Pairs** asks you to select sets of images. Do you choose by race, gender, or profession? **Try Changing Places** mirrors your own face above different outfits: a cheerleader costume, a corporate suit, overalls. In **Images That Stay with Us** you are reminded of stereotype images encountered from childhood on: "Fat men are jolly . . . Asians are sinister . . . Women are helpless." **It's So Easy to Misjudge** illustrates how we often categorize and make false assumptions about people based on their appearance.

Sometimes we encounter people who seem to reinforce the images we grow up with, as in **Are We Real or Stereotypes?** Pop-up heads speak in confusing cacophony: "In 1492 my people welcomed Columbus. Big mistake. . . ." laments a Native American. "I very confused. American dream *big* nightmare," says an Asian-American immigrant in broken English. "But you also confused. . . ." he aptly states.

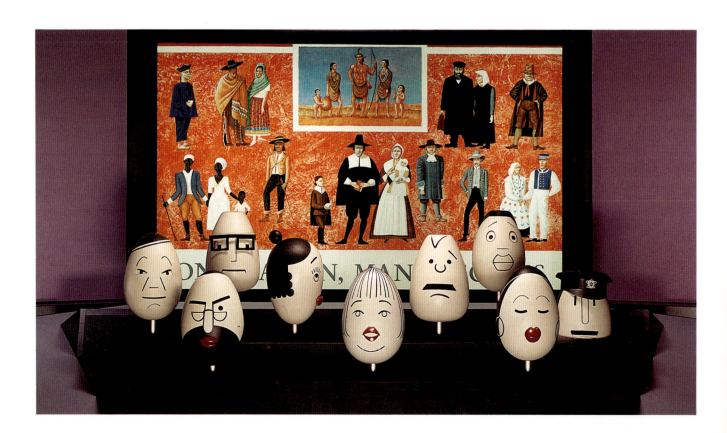

TIMELINE
UNDERSTANDING THE LOS ANGELES RIOTS

On March 3, 1991, an African American, Rodney King, was arrested after a car chase in Los Angeles. A group of white police officers severely beat him. Television stations across the nation subsequently broadcast parts of an amateur videotape of the beating. On April 29, 1992, a predominantly white jury in suburban Simi Valley acquitted the officers, triggering America's worst riots in the 20th century. In four days of lawlessness in Los Angeles, 52 people died, 2,400 were injured, and 20,000 lost their jobs. Total damage was estimated at $1 billion.

What *really* caused the riots? In the **Tolerancenter** you explore the events surrounding them and confront the disturbing questions left in their aftermath. At interactive multimedia stations you view a short film about the riots and follow twelve

ABOVE: *Though the physical violence of the Los Angeles riots eventually abated, rage against injustice and racial prejudice continued to smolder among its residents.*

chronological "Timeline" segments, which take you from the Rodney King beating through efforts to rebuild Los Angeles.

The exhibit poses a series of multiple-choice questions: *Can the beating of Rodney King ever be justified? Did the looting look like fun? Were store owners right to take up arms?* The computer tabulates your answers and shows how your feelings compare with those of other people. The exhibit leaves you with a better understanding of the ethnic and economic issues that we must all confront to maintain peace in our communities.

ABOVE: *Meet Video Heads Joe Cool, Mr. Normal, and Miss Uptight. You follow their on-screen thought processes, which reflect the heavy influence of advertising and other media.*

We often look to our idols for guidance—surely *they* know what is right and wrong. But look again at **Video Heads.** The "perfectly clear" views that **Joe Cool, Miss Uptight,** and **Mr. Normal** have of the world reveal that we all see things differently.

WORDS VERSUS THOUGHTS

Tempered by reason, words help us to communicate. But when reason is abandoned and emotion takes over, words create barriers and can incite us to violence.

Many people fail to recognize the racism or bigotry in their own words. The video presentation **Me . . . A Bigot?** vividly illustrates this problem. People at a multiethnic gathering make insulting and intolerant remarks about others but seem unable to recognize intolerance in themselves.

People's "tolerant" words often mask intolerant feelings. In **What We Say, What We Think** you view scenarios of typical conversations, such

ABOVE: *Popular American icons from the early 1900s through the present adorn the Revolving Drums exhibit. Cars, Broadway theater, advertising slogans, and sports and screen idols—how have they influenced our thinking?*

ABOVE: *This cartoon story shows how mounting resentment and verbal aggression between ethnic groups can lead to violence.*

as a male executive reviewing a female colleague's work performance. The spoken words are complimentary, but his true thoughts are revealed as being sexist and bigoted.

When our negative thoughts become spoken words, we reach a higher level of intolerance. **Dangerous Words** asks you to identify words that have negative connotations. In **Words Break More than Bones** a whisper gallery directs emotionally tainted words at you. Hateful slurs fill the chamber: "Lousy gook . . . Redneck . . . Whatcha gonna do about it, Jew boy?" With every taunt the line between words and physical aggression draws ever closer.

CROSSING THE LINE

It is easier than most people think for negative thoughts to lead to violent acts. Just inside the **Prejudiced** door a slide presentation depicts the threshold of violence. Its message flashes across the wall: **The Potential for Violence Is Within All of Us.** Anyone with prejudice (meaning all of us, as the two entry doors emphasize) has the potential to cross the thin line between feelings of hatred and violent acts.

The **Cartoon Wall** illustrates this potential between groups of African-American and Latino high school students. The two groups face off, beginning with verbal assaults and ending with two teens lying on the ground, bleeding from knife wounds. The carpet in the exhibit area turns from blue to red, graphically illustrating the line between verbal and physical violence. In the red-carpeted section a changing exhibit shows the different faces of violence—from gangs, to a mob, to threatening paramilitary police.

AM I NOT A MAN AND A BROTHER

ABOVE & BELOW: *This chronological mural records three levels of important events in American history, from colonization to the present: landmark historical events, episodes of intolerance, and acts that reflect individual and government efforts to promote tolerance.*

THE AMERICAN EXPERIENCE

After participating in these interactive exhibits about how we think and act, you trace the history of intolerance in the United States. You also learn of governmental acts and individual initiatives that have been responsible for positive change. On the 60-foot **American History Wall** a chronological mural graphically displays landmark events, acts of intolerance, and struggles for human justice of the last four centuries. **Ain't You Gotta Right?**, a 16-screen video wall, highlights the crucial years in the civil rights struggle in America and the inspirational story of Dr. Martin Luther King, Jr. (see page 22).

It may seem that our country has taken major steps toward eliminating hatred. Yet it thrives within our borders, as you discover from **The Other America**, a large, computerized map. The touch-screen computer allows you to review more than 250 hate groups and their current activities throughout the United States.

THE PERSUADERS

The **American History Wall** merges into a series of familiar and persuasive American media icons from the 1920s to the present, all displayed

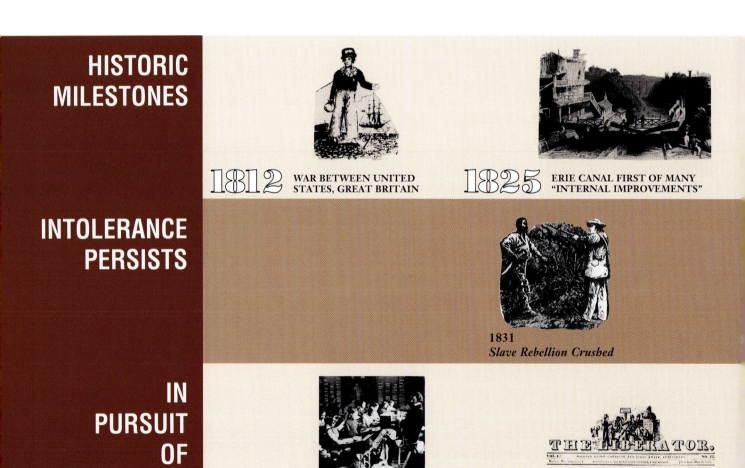

HISTORIC MILESTONES

1812 WAR BETWEEN UNITED STATES, GREAT BRITAIN

1825 ERIE CANAL FIRST OF MANY "INTERNAL IMPROVEMENTS"

INTOLERANCE PERSISTS

1831
Slave Rebellion Crushed

IN PURSUIT OF TOLERANCE

1821
Troy Female Seminary Founded

THE LIBERATOR.

1831
Newpaper Urges Freedom for Slaves

Just as our thoughts affect our language, so language can be used to affect our thoughts . . . and eventually, our actions and behavior.

ABOVE: *Demagogues effectively use language to manipulate the emotions, thoughts, and eventually the actions, of masses of people.*

on **Revolving Drums.** These lead to a dramatic, multiscreen exhibit. As dozens of **Persuaders**—statesmen, actors, and other influential people—speak to you, the **Manipulator** looms into full view. He pressures you to return to his control: "So you think that just 'cause you've been through these tolerance exhibits, you can make up your own mind?" He ends by giving up all responsibility.

After the **Manipulator** fades, a probing question flashes before you: *Who is responsible?* The answer is dramatically revealed in many different languages: *You are!*

1846 MEXICAN WAR FUELS CONTINENTAL EXPANSION

1849 GOLD RUSH LEADS TO CALIFORNIA STATEHOOD

1844
Philadelphia Religious Riot

MEXICANS' RIGHTS ABUSED

1850
Movement Against Foreign-borns

1852
UNCLE TOM'S CABIN

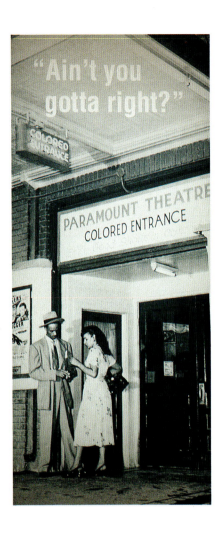

ABOVE: *Although the Declaration of Independence professed equality for all U.S. citizens, people of color were forced to live in a separate, unequal society well into the 1960s. A series of visual displays and a multiscreen film document the struggle for civil rights in our nation's history.*

"I Have a Dream"

An Individual Who Made a Difference

Born in 1929 in Atlanta, Georgia, the Reverend Martin Luther King, Jr., became a leader of hundreds of thousands of people in protesting segregation and inequality and in demanding the basic human rights that had been denied to individuals on the basis of skin color.

Dr. King's leadership began in December 1955 after Rosa Parks, a 42-year-old seamstress in Montgomery, Alabama, refused to give up her bus seat to a white man. King led a nonviolent boycott of the city's bus system until the buses were integrated nearly a year later.

King founded the Southern Christian Leadership Conference in Atlanta in January 1957. He then embarked on a decade-long journey of speeches, marches, demonstrations, and negotiations with leaders of our nation. On August 28, 1963, millions watched on television as King led more than 250,000 people in the Freedom March in Washington, D.C.

Dr. King's efforts achieved international recognition, and he was awarded the Nobel Peace Prize in 1964. Until his assassination four years later, King continued leading protests for voting rights and racial justice, including famous demonstrations in Selma, Alabama. The civil rights movement resulted in new legislation that brought African Americans and other minorities closer to the equality they deserve as citizens of the United States.

LEFT: *The Reverend Martin Luther King, Jr., at the March on Washington. Under his leadership the civil rights movement showed the world the awesome power of nonviolent protest to achieve human rights.*

BELOW: *In 1960–1962 civil rights workers and students staged nonviolent sit-ins in southern cities to protest segregation of public facilities. The peaceful demonstrators were often met with hostility, anger, and violence.*

LEFT: *In 1963 Dr. King led a series of nonviolent protests in Birmingham, Alabama. Eugene ("Bull") Connor, the city's director of public safety, authorized his forces to attack the demonstrators, including children and college students, with police dogs and fire hoses.*

ABOVE: *Panels in this exhibit show news accounts from previous centuries then flip to frighteningly similar accounts from recent years. A fanatical leader calls for "ethnic cleansing"—thousands of people are killed. Has anything changed?*

CHOICE EQUALS RESPONSIBILITY

These Headlines Could Be Today's Headlines shows that thousand-year-old news resembles today's: holy wars, massacres, discrimination. Why is this?

One major reason is the ability of powerful leaders to sway their followers. In the **Demagogues** panel you see how words can excite people and win support by making emotional appeals to prejudice. Given the right circumstances, demagogues can incite people to large-scale acts of aggression and violence anywhere in the world.

Across the hall **The Immigrant Experience** mural reminds us that, as new waves of immigrants arrive, we must continue working toward eliminating rising extremes of intolerance.

The **Tolerancenter**'s parting words convey its ultimate message: though people and the media can exert a great deal of power, we can *choose* not to succumb. Otherwise, we risk repeating an era of extreme inhumanity, such as the Holocaust, which is portrayed in the next section of the museum.

BELOW: *History shows that most acts of mass aggression result from the powerful influence of demagogues.*

IT IS CALLED GENOCIDE

ABOVE: *Pol Pot and the Khmer Rouge waged a monumental reign of horror in Cambodia in the mid-1970s. The result: over 1.5 million Cambodians were murdered.*

Sometimes intolerance rises to such a level that a group of people attempts to annihilate another. The term for this large-scale murder was coined by Raphael Lemkin, a Jewish jurist, in 1933. He called it "genocide."

As the clearest and most terrifying example of genocide, the Holocaust was neither the first nor the last in our century. The ten-minute film *It Is Called Genocide* highlights three genocides that were committed after 1900.

The first wide-scale modern genocide occurred from 1915 through 1918, when between 500,000 and 1,000,000 Armenians were killed. Nearly another million were forced to flee their homelands. This was the murderous culmination of a history of intolerance toward ethnic Armenians in the Ottoman Empire.

In the 1970s Pol Pot and the Khmer Rouge murdered one-sixth of Cambodia's population—more than 1,500,000 people. The victims included those whom Pol Pot feared would oppose his revolution: former members of the government and army, religious and minority ethnic groups, the middle-class, and the educated.

Finally, we learn that the term *genocide* also applies to the many thousands of native people who are dying all over Latin America. Massacres, government indifference, starvation, and disease contribute to the annihilation of the Indians.

BEIT HASHOAH

THE COURAGE
TO REMEMBER

■

From 1933 to 1945 the Nazis murdered 6,000,000 Jews and millions of others. This tragedy, called the Holocaust, represents the world's most overwhelming example of intolerance. **Beit Hashoah,** "House of the Holocaust," educates visitors to help prevent such a disaster from ever recurring. In a journey through history you become an "eyewitness" to the events of the Holocaust.

A film sets the mood for the Roaring Twenties, a period of optimism and change. The narrator invites you to "imagine you are going back in time—to that Golden Age of the 1920s—to Berlin, a great city, right in the heart of Europe." An invitation to take your **Photo Passport Card** for this part of the museum draws you closer to the experience.

ABOVE: *This street scene brings you to 1932 Berlin, on the eve of Hitler's rise to power. Eavesdrop on conversations at this elegant café, then flash forward as the narrator reveals the characters' futures. Some play important roles in the Nazi regime, while others fall victim to Nazi persecution.*

PAGES 26–27: *New arrivals marked for death walk toward the gas chamber at a Nazi death camp.*

GERMANY AFTER WORLD WAR I

At the **Designer's Studio** and **Researcher's Office,** you are introduced to the political and economic climate of post–World War I Germany and Berlin.

Berlin was one of Europe's most modern, fashionable cities, but it was also plagued by political unrest. Many Germans felt humiliated after losing the war and wanted to restore the nation to its former glory. Extremists pressed for immediate change. One such group was the National Socialist German Workers Party (Nazis), who blamed Germany's defeat on the Jews. At first only a few people listened to such extreme ideas. But Hitler's forceful, impassioned—almost hypnotic—speeches eventually mesmerized audiences and swept them under his control.

In 1923 Germany was struck by a great economic depression. Hitler took advantage of the atmosphere and again blamed the Jews, and the communists as well. His fiery speeches and the Nazi slogans rallied more and more people to side with the Nazi party.

WHY THE JEWS?

When Hitler blamed the Jews for Germany's problems, he was reviving an ancient prejudice. Because of their distinct culture and religion, European Jews had been continual targets for nearly 2,000 years. The Nazis resurrected old patterns of persecution to promote their ultimate goal:

This passport card is the key
to the personal story of

Eva Beem

RIGHT: *When you begin the Holocaust tour, you receive a Photo Passport Card bearing the name of an innocent child who experienced the Holocaust. You update your passport at various stages along the tour, receiving more information about the child's circumstances. At the end you receive a one-page biography, which includes the child's ultimate fate.*

a *Judenfrei* (Jew-free) Europe. Antisemitic propaganda, such as newspapers, posters, and games, began appearing all over Germany.

The Nazis also spread their racist philosophy that Aryans (white northern Europeans) were superior and Jews and others were subhuman. Displayed next to the **Researcher's Office** are illustrations from some scientists' published theories that classified people by race.

1932 BERLIN

Lively music from Bertholt Brecht's *Threepenny Opera* accompanies you into a typical **Street Scene** of 1932 Berlin. Among the shops here is a bookstore, which displays Adolf Hitler's popular *Mein Kampf.* Much of the book details his hatred of the Jews.

Hitler was now an influential politician, and he ran for president of Germany in 1932, as you see from election posters. He lost the election . . . that time.

In 1932 few people could imagine what would really happen if Hitler were in charge. In the **Café,** a popular gathering spot for Berliners, you overhear typical conversations of the time. A young American, for example, attempts to convince her Jewish friend Ilse to move to Chicago. "You worry too much!" says Ilse, who believes her family has earned enough respect in Berlin to escape harm. The narrator reports that Ilse and her husband were later deported to Latvia by the Nazis and murdered.

BELOW: *Conversation among a researcher, a designer, and a historian provides background about events and information on the visual displays and exhibits.*

ABOVE: *When he assumed power in 1933, Hitler called for citizens to boycott all Jewish-owned businesses and shops. Graffiti with the word* Jude *(Jew) and the Star of David indicated the targets.*

ABOVE: *In May 1933 the Nazis banned and burned thousands of books whose contents allegedly conflicted with Nazi philosophy.*

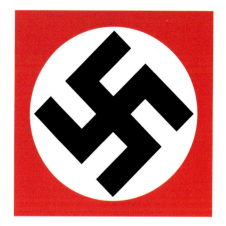

ABOVE: *The swastika was the symbol of the Nazi party.*

OPPOSITE: *Julius Streicher, Nazi propagandist, published antisemitic literature, including this children's storybook, which portrays Jews as shameful, sneaky, ugly scoundrels and Germans as proud, strong, and handsome masters.*

HITLER AND THE NAZIS COME TO POWER

Back in the **Designer's Studio** you begin following the events that would soon change the destiny of millions of people.

On January 30, 1933, Hitler became chancellor of Germany. Within weeks he had taken the first steps toward total dictatorship: he suspended civil liberties and suppressed all opposition, sending thousands of dissidents to the Dachau concentration camp. He urged people to boycott all Jewish businesses and shops. He dismissed Jews from the civil service, expelled Jewish teachers and students from the universities, and banned the books of great writers and philosophers.

The 1935 Nuremberg Laws stripped Jews of their citizenship and other basic rights. In the months that followed, thousands tried to leave Germany, but most had nowhere to go. Most countries were unwilling to accept a large number of Jewish refugees. The Jews were trapped.

The Rise of Nazism chronicles the party's increasing popularity in the 1930s. As you view the Nuremberg rally film on six life-size screens, you sense the emotion of the giant Nazi marches, demonstrations, and parades that swept masses of Germans into Hitler's power. The *Third Reich*, or "Third Empire," boasted a glorious future that would last 1,000 years and offered Germans renewed pride in themselves and their country. Hitler had succeeded in convincing millions that they were the "master race."

Archival film footage and animated maps relate the historic events of Nazi expansion. In March 1938 the Nazis marched into Vienna and declared Austria part of the Greater German Reich. The persecution of Jews began there immediately. That September Hitler forced Czechoslovakia to give up part of its territory. Hitler was at the height of his popularity.

THE NIGHTMARE BEGINS

Kristallnacht occurred during the night of November 9–10, 1938 (see page 32). Hundreds of synagogues were attacked and burned, and Jewish shops were vandalized and looted. During this massive pogrom (antisemitic riot) 30,000 Jewish men were sent to concentration camps. The stage was now set for Hitler to escalate his war against the Jews.

On September 1, 1939, Germany invaded Poland, and Britain and France declared war on Germany. World War II had begun.

The reign of terror had also begun. The Nazis almost immediately murdered more than 120,000 Polish Jews and forced hundreds of thousands into ghettos. The Nazi war machine soon overtook France and part of the Soviet Union. By the beginning of 1942 millions of Jews were trapped in the Nazi net.

KRISTALLNACHT

Kristallnacht, or "The Night of Broken Glass," refers to the organized, anti-Jewish riots in Germany and Austria, on the night of November 9–10 in 1938. At least 91 Jews were killed. Rioters burned hundreds of synagogues and vandalized and ransacked over 7,000 Jewish shops, businesses, and homes. Kristallnacht is especially significant because it marked a major turning point in the Nazi campaign against the Jews.

Nazi antisemitic policy began with the systematic, legal, economic, and social disenfranchisement of Jews in Germany. As part of their plan the Nazis had earlier deported an estimated 18,000 Polish Jews on October 28, 1938. The deportees were refused entry into Poland and were stranded at the border. On hearing that his family was among this group, Herschel Grynszpan, a 17-year-old student in Paris, shot Ernst vom Rath, third secretary of the German Embassy.

The Nazis used this act of revenge as a welcome pretext to launch a large-scale, organized attack on the Jewish people. Reich security leader Reinhard Heydrich gave official instructions to police to incite riots against Jews throughout Germany and Austria.

Heydrich's orders resulted in the first violent pogrom (antisemitic riot) on Western European soil in hundreds of years. On that fateful evening Nazis stepped from political antisemitism to the next stage of their overall plan: overt, complete destruction of all Jewish life in the Third Reich.

RIGHT: *During Kristallnacht, a Nazi-ordered antisemitic riot in Germany and Austria on November 9–10, 1938, over 250 synagogues burned, including this one in Berlin.*

ABOVE: *Hitler gained popularity in the 1930s through massive rallies, parades, and mesmerizing speeches.*

WANNSEE: THE FINAL SOLUTION TO THE JEWISH QUESTION

Hitler wanted to rid Europe of Jews, but how was he to achieve this goal efficiently? Reichsmarschall Hermann Goering, second in command to Hitler, ordered SS General Reinhard Heydrich to prepare a secret plan. Heydrich and 14 top officials met in a villa by Berlin's Lake Wannsee on January 20, 1942.

At the museum's re-creation of the **Wannsee Conference,** you eavesdrop on the secret meeting. The officials discuss extermination methods and agree on Hitler's Final Solution—the systematic murder of the 11,000,000 Jews of Europe. Polish Jews would go first; Jews from other countries would be deported to death camps after transportation problems were resolved.

ROUNDUPS AND ESCAPE

The following exhibits detail the roundups and deportations, which intensified during 1942. Jews were singled out for total annihilation; millions of Gypsies, homosexuals, dissidents, communists, intellectuals, the mentally ill and handicapped, and many others were also Nazi victims.

The Nazis' antisemitic allies all over Europe facilitated the roundups. German *Einsatzgruppen* (mobile killing units) swept across Eastern Europe, slaughtering as many Jews as possible. In Lithuania and parts of the Soviet Union, local police enthusiastically and brutally participated in massacres.

ABOVE: *The Nazis also targeted Gypsies for elimination, like this mother and child in 1940 at the Lackenberg transit camp in Burgenland, Austria.*

JEWISH RESISTANCE

After seeing photos of Jews being marched to their deaths, many people assume that they did not fight back. On the contrary—despite oppression, disease, and starvation, Jews throughout occupied Europe resisted, revealing the highest achievement of the human spirit.

Jewish resistance took many forms. Children smuggled food and other forbidden items into the ghettos. Elders conducted secret religious services, despite Nazi bans. Merely staying alive was a form of resistance: the Nazis tortured and killed Jews for the mildest infractions. Occasionally the Nazis murdered entire families and villages in reprisal for a single act of Jewish resistance.

Some Jewish men and women formed resistance groups. Though badly outnumbered and poorly armed, they blew up railway lines and supply trains and did everything possible to hinder the Germans. Armed Jewish uprisings occurred in many ghettos and death camps. Most who revolted against the Germans were caught and murdered. The most famous uprising took place in the Warsaw Ghetto.

On October 12, 1940, the Nazis established the ghetto. Eventually, they forced almost 500,000 Polish Jews to live there in an area smaller than two square miles. Thousands died from starvation and disease. Mass deportations to death camps began in July 1942. When the Nazis temporarily halted deportations that September, fewer than 100,000 Jews remained.

In April 1943 when the Germans resumed the deportations, they met courageous resistance. The Jews knew victory was impossible, but they managed for an entire month to hold off a well-equipped and much-larger German force. On May 16 the German commander reported that "the Jewish quarter of Warsaw was no more."

Though the Nazis razed the ghetto, they were unable to erase the memory of Jewish bravery and dignity in the face of certain death.

ABOVE: *Before World War II Warsaw was one of the world's largest Jewish communities. By 1941 the Nazis crammed almost half a million Polish Jews into a ghetto of less than two square miles. Here, Jews are being forced to build the ghetto wall.*

ABOVE: *Life in the ghetto meant starvation, disease, and unbelievable hardship. But the Jews struggled to provide education, health care, soup for the needy, and a cultural life for residents.*

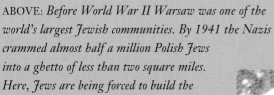

LEFT: *The Nazis placed strict bans on religious activities. Jews conducted clandestine prayer services and study sessions, such as this service being held in the Warsaw Ghetto.*

RIGHT: *Jewish men, women, and children resisted Nazi oppression in every way possible. Thousands were able to escape and join armed partisan groups.*

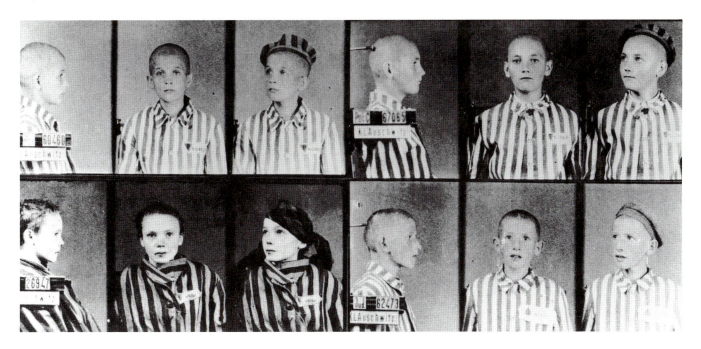

Escape—legal or illegal—was futile for most Jews. Only a few were accepted by other countries. Earlier, the United States refused entry to nearly a thousand Jewish refugees who had fled Germany on the ocean liner *St. Louis.* They were forced to return to Europe.

Though Jews faced certain doom, they resisted in every way possible. Two poignant exhibits, the **Warsaw Ghetto** and **Jewish Resistance,** portray the inhuman conditions of the ghettos and heroic attempts to resist the Nazi oppressors (see page 34).

1942–1945: MASS MURDER

A large **Railway Map** shows the vast transportation network used to deport millions of Jews from all over occupied Europe to hundreds of concentration camps. Crammed into cattle cars, many died along the way.

Those who arrived alive were either murdered immediately or forced into slave labor. Thousands were gassed daily; others died from disease, starvation, and Nazi brutality. By 1945 some 6,000,000 European Jews had been slain.

AUSCHWITZ: THE DEATH FACTORY

As you step through a replica of the actual **Gates of Auschwitz,** you trace the steps taken by more than 1,500,000 inmates at the largest Nazi death camp. A model and the adjacent diorama reveal the enormity and stark, inhuman atmosphere. A floodlight sweeps across the darkened barracks. Smoke from one of the four crematoriums rises in the background.

From there you continue through one of two **Tunnels,** labeled **Able-Bodied** and **Children and Others,** which brings to mind the selection process many underwent upon arrival at the camp. Those deemed able to work stayed alive, at least for a short time. Others—children, the elderly, the handicapped or ill—were sent to the gas chambers.

The **Tunnels** lead to a dimly lit chamber, the **Hall of Testimony,** where you listen to personal stories of Holocaust survivors (see page 40).

ABOVE: *Those children who were not killed immediately were photographed and numbered on arrival at the camps.*

OPPOSITE: *Museum visitors pass through a replica of the gates of Auschwitz, the largest Nazi death camp. More than a million people died after passing through these gates.*

BELOW: *The Nazis forced Jews to wear a yellow star at all times for easy identification.*

The Enduring Human Spirit

During the Holocaust the human spirit proved amazingly durable. It shines in the story and words of Anne Frank, the young Jewish girl whose diary was published after the war: "I think it will all come right, that this cruelty too will end. . . ." Hope and faith are also reflected in the drawings and paintings retrieved from the Theresienstadt Ghetto camp, many of which were created by children.

Even toward the end of the war, when conditions were the worst, the human spirit endured. Three days after the American troops liberated the Mauthausen camp, three women inmates presented the commander with a handmade American flag, pieced together from salvaged cloth. The flag is on permanent display at the museum—a symbol of renewed hope.

ABOVE: *Inmates at the Mauthausen concentration camp sewed this flag in secrecy during the final days of World War II. It contains 56 stars (the inmates couldn't remember the exact number of states) and 13 stripes.*

ABOVE & LEFT: *The tragic story of Anne Frank and her family, who spent two years hiding from the Nazis in a Dutch office building, became world renowned when Anne's diary was published. It symbolizes the remarkable beauty, strength, and simplicity of the human spirit in the face of adversity. On display at the museum is correspondence, written entirely in English in early 1940, of Anne and her sister Margot and their pen pals in Iowa.*

ABOVE: *The Nazis created the Theresienstadt Ghetto camp to deceive the world. On the surface it appeared to be an autonomous Jewish city with cabarets, schools, banks, and a rich cultural life. In reality it was a transit station for death camps. The museum's archival collection includes numerous artworks created by Theresienstadt residents.*

THE HALL OF TESTIMONY

It is difficult for those of us who did not experience the Holocaust personally to imagine the atrocities perpetrated by the Nazis. The **Hall of Testimony,** perhaps the most moving section of the museum, attempts to give visitors a sense of both the despair and hope that the Jews and other victims experienced during the Holocaust.

As you stand beneath steel girders in a dark, concrete hall, you listen to the first-person testimonies of victims, perpetrators, and witnesses. A series of video-photo montages accompanies the stories.

The stories vary from that of a woman who watched her newborn niece thrown from a hospital window, to a description of a gas chamber scene from the Nazi perspective, to a woman who survived a mass shooting and escaped to the forest.

The story of Roza Robota, a courageous young woman at Auschwitz, represents the Jews' fighting spirit that refused to buckle under Nazi pressure. The Robota family was brought to the camp in November 1942. Roza was 21 years old. On the day they arrived she watched the rest of her family walk to the gas chambers.

Still at Auschwitz two years later, Roza found an opportunity to avenge her family's deaths. She and other inmates who were forced to work at a

BELOW: *The concrete walls and steel girders in the Hall of Testimony evoke the inhuman feeling of the Nazi camps.*

munitions plant smuggled out dynamite for the camp's resistance organization. On October 7, 1944, the resistance blew a crematorium to pieces. Five SS men died. Six hundred inmates escaped; most were caught and shot in a few days.

The SS tortured Roza to learn who was responsible. She betrayed no one. Her last words, scribbled on a piece of paper just before she was hanged, were *"Chazak V'Ehmatz"*—"Be strong and brave."

In another story a father voices similar words to his young son, as they sit together in a cattle car bound for Auschwitz: "We must be strong now, more than ever."

In our scroll of agony, not one small detail can be omitted. . . . We are now undergoing terrible tribulations and the sun has grown dark for us at noon.

Chaim A. Kaplan
The Warsaw Diary

ABOVE: *Schutzpass. In an attempt to rescue Hungarian Jews from deportation, Swedish envoy to Budapest, Raoul Wallenberg, issued tens of thousands of provisional, or "protective," passports. These passports were honored for the most part, allowing Jews to remain and live in special housing.*

WHO WAS RESPONSIBLE?

From the **Hall of Testimony** you encounter the final series of exhibits. The first poses the question, **Who Was Responsible?** Many share responsibility for the Holocaust: fanatics, those who blindly followed orders, intolerant bigots, world leaders, and ordinary people who remained silent.

The **Wall of the Righteous** pays tribute to courageous non-Jews who risked their own lives to help Jews. Forty-nine representative accounts of human valor appear on the wall—such stories as those of a Ukrainian farmer who hid a Jewish family in his stable and the Romanian mayor who halted the deportation of 20,000 Jews. A video monitor continuously scrolls the names of the more than 8,000 righteous.

After the final update of your **Photo Passport Card,** you pause at the **Global Situation Room,** where monitors flash up-to-the-minute information on current worldwide incidents of antisemitism and intolerance (see page 43). When you compare these bulletins with the events leading to the Holocaust, is it farfetched to imagine it could happen again?

THE WORLD THAT WAS

Your journey through time concludes with a glimpse of Jewish life before the Holocaust. The film *Echoes That Remain* shows the rich, vibrant culture of former Jewish communities.

The film combines hundreds of rare archival photographs and previously unseen film footage that was shot on location at the sites of former Jewish communities in Czechoslovakia, Poland, Hungary, and Romania.

LEFT: *After Kristallnacht in 1938 a group of desperate parents wrote to Lillie Herrmann Philipp, a German living in London who dedicated herself to helping Jewish children escape from Germany. The parents asked Mrs. Philipp to help place their children in English foster homes, schools, or jobs. Their letters are on display in the museum's archives.*

THE GLOBAL SITUATION ROOM

Unfortunately, hatred did not die in 1945 in the bunker with Hitler. In the **Global Situation Room** you see that acts of intolerance still occur worldwide. This state-of-the-art newsroom is connected to international news services, news wires, and electronic research networks. These provide up-to-the-minute information about bigotry, antisemitism, prejudice, and intolerance around the globe.

Through a glass wall you see Simon Wiesenthal Center research staff compiling and analyzing details of human rights violations. Overhead monitors flash bulletins with related news items or live coverage of events. Current international news releases are available to you outside the room.

The **Global Situation Room** reveals that the BEIT HASHOAH ■ MUSEUM OF TOLERANCE is a living entity. Monitoring the activities of human rights violations links the atrocities of the past with those of the present and reminds us of our continuous need to be on the alert for acts of injustice and intolerance wherever they occur.

ABOVE: *Fifty years after the Holocaust many hate groups, such as neo-Nazis, still terrorize foreigners and minority groups all over the world.*

BELOW: *Within the glass walls of the Global Situation Room, researchers compile up-to-the-minute data on human rights violations around the world.*

ANTISEMITISM AND
THE FINAL SOLUTION'

ז

ACCESS TO HISTORY

■

The museum's **Multimedia Learning Center** and archival collections offer visitors unique perspectives and comprehensive information on the events surrounding the Holocaust.

THE MULTIMEDIA LEARNING CENTER

The second floor of the museum is designed for personalized research on the Holocaust, World War II, and related topics. Over 5,700 separate entries are accessed by computer through touch-screen technology. Fifty-seven thousand photographs— from the world's leading archives and private collections—and rare documents and maps, along with live video testimony from eyewitnesses to history, are available to the visitor at the touch of a finger. Thirty-two computer learning stations provide a multidimensional view of events never before available.

PAGES 44–45: *The Multimedia Learning Center is an outstanding computerized source of Holocaust-related research. It provides immediate access to thousands of documents, photographs, maps, and personal testimonies on a multimedia, interactive videodisc system.*

Main topics include Major Battles and Strategies of World War II, Antisemitism and the Final Solution, the Jews, the Nazis, Righteous Among the Nations, Resistance and Rescue, World Response, and After the War.

The **Multimedia Learning Center**'s approach enables every visitor to utilize the collective expertise of Time-Life Books, the Macmillan *Encyclopedia of the Holocaust*, the *Encyclopedia Judaica*, and other authoritative sources.

THEY WILL ALWAYS BE HEARD:
ARTIFACTS & DOCUMENTS OF THE HOLOCAUST

The high-tech environment of the Learning Center shares the 8,500-square-foot second floor with the museum's compelling exhibit of artifacts and documents. Among other items, the collection includes:

- Correspondence of Anne Frank and her sister Margot and their American pen pals in 1940
- Rare works of art, including a magnificent collection of drawings from the Theresienstadt Ghetto camp
- A bunk from the Majdanek death camp
- A megillah scroll recovered from the ruins of the Warsaw Ghetto
- A 56-star American flag secretly sewn by the inmates of the Mauthausen concentration camp
- An original Schutzpass, prepared and issued by Raoul Wallenberg
- The signed confession of the chief SS doctor at Majdanek
- A collection of nearly 150 artifacts from Auschwitz

The BEIT HASHOAH ▪ MUSEUM OF TOLERANCE also features a number of special installations. Each exhibit encourages visitors to contemplate issues related to the museum's themes.

ART FOR INSPIRATION

Intriguing works of art throughout the museum offer unique perspectives on the Holocaust. Among the most prominent is the magnificent **Tower of Witness,** a sculptural monument that rises 96 feet from the main floor to the top of the dome. The sculpture was designed to contain 2,480 photographs, courtesy of Ann Weiss and the State Museum of Auschwitz-Birkenau. These were among the few precious items that Auschwitz victims were able to bring on their journey to the camp. The tower bears witness to the sanctity of life and the endurance of the human spirit.

Adjacent to the museum building is the 16,000-square-foot **Memorial Plaza,** which honors all the victims of the Holocaust and the related themes of courage, hope, and rebirth. An 18-foot menorah in the center of the plaza reflects the continuity of Jewish civilization despite efforts

LEFT: *History comes alive at your fingertips: touch a button and view rare photographs, documents, maps, and video footage, accompanied by explanatory narrative and text.*

BELOW: *Visitors are welcome to conduct their own historical research using state-of-the-art technology at 32 computer learning stations.*

LEFT: *This SS Totenkopf (Death's Head) cap and instruments of torture used by the Nazis were found at Auschwitz in the 1950s.*

RIGHT: *An original wooden bunk bed from the Majdanek death camp.*